NOT-SO-ORDINARY SCIENCE

GET MESSY WITH SCIENCE!

PROJECTS THAT OOZE, FOAM, AND MORE

by Elsie Olson

CAPSTONE PRESS
a capstone imprint

Dabble Lab is published by Capstone Press, an imprint of Capstone.
1710 Roe Crest Drive, North Mankato, Minnesota 56003
capstonepub.com

Copyright © 2023 by Capstone. All rights reserved. No part of this publication may be reproduced in whole or in part, or stored in a retrieval system, or transmitted in any form or by any means, electronic, mechanical, photocopying, recording, or otherwise, without written permission of the publisher.

Library of Congress Cataloging-in-Publication Data is available on the Library of Congress website.
ISBN: 9781666342178 (hardcover)
ISBN: 9781666342185 (ebook PDF)

Summary: Do you like to get messy? These science projects are for you! Create slippery slimes and frothy foams. Have a blast making colorful explosions. Then, learn the science behind each marvelous mess!

Image Credits
Shutterstock: kubais, Front Cover (blue paint), ONYXprj (background), Front Cover, Back Cover, schankz (splotch), Front Cover, 3, 16, Vera NewSib (watermelon), Front Cover, 20, 32, Africa Studio (cornstarch), 4, 14, Apple_Mac (measuring cups & spoons), 4, 8, arsslawa, 4 (rubber bands), Elizabeth A.Cummings (food coloring), 4, 6, 10, 26, endeavor (mixing bowl), 4, 28, focal point, 4 (baking soda), J u n e (mixing spoon), 4, 10, 28, Mega Pixel, 4 (school glue), 12 (clear glue), Natakorn Ruangrit, 4 (scissors), stuar, 4 (dish soap), Worraratch Chinboon (liquid starch), 4, 13, 29, Andrei Dubadzel, 6 (yeast), Noel V. Baebler, 6 (hydrogen peroxide), kenary820, 8 (saline solution), diy13, 9 (white bottle), sulit.photos, 14 (borax), Love the wind, 15 (glitter), oksana2010, 16 (chalk), VR/IRUS (hammer), 16, 17, New Africa, 17 (baking soda), Vandathai, 17 (chalk powder), Ascannio, 18 (putty), JUN3, 18 (tape), jultud, 21 (safety glasses), Napat, 22 (funnel), wk1003mike, 22 (deflated balloons), timquo, 23 (filled balloons), Yellow Cat, 24 (blue toy dinosaur), akiyoko, 25 (acrylic paint), Dmitriy Kazitsyn, 26 (ice pack), Olha Solodenko, 26 (blow-dryer)

Design Elements
Shutterstock: MicroOne (gauges), WhiteBarbie (calendar date)
All project photos shot by Mighty Media, Inc.

Editorial Credits
Editor: Jessica Rusick
Designer: Aruna Rangarajan

All internet sites appearing in back matter were available and accurate when this book was sent to press.

The publisher and the author shall not be liable for any damages allegedly arising from the information in this book, and they specifically disclaim any liability from the use or application of any of the contents of this book.

Printed and bound in the USA. PO4882

TABLE OF CONTENTS

Make a Mess! 4

Foaming Swamp Monster 6

Slime Bubbles 8

Hot & Cold Water Stack 10

Ooey Gooey Rocks 12

Glitter Bouncy Balls 14

Chalk Bomb 16

Fierce Fountain 18

Exploding Watermelon 20

Paint Splatter Art 22

Icky Tar Pit 24

Color-Shifting Slime 26

Sculptable Sand 28

Squeeze & Splat Eggs 30

Read More 32

Internet Sites 32

MAKE A MESS!

What happens when experiments explode and chemistry goes kaboom? It turns out marvelously messy science projects also happen to be fantastically fun. So grab your goggles, put on your lab coat, and cover your work area.

THINGS ARE ABOUT TO GET MESSY!

GENERAL SUPPLIES & TOOLS

baking soda

cornstarch

dish soap

food coloring

liquid starch

measuring cups & spoons

mixing bowl & spoon

rubber bands

school glue

scissors

TIPS & TRICKS

FOLLOW THESE SIMPLE TIPS TO STAY SAFE AND HAVE FUN!

- **Read all the steps** and gather all your supplies before starting a project.

- **Wear eye protection** when working with explosions.

- **Wash your hands** after handling slime.

- **These projects are messy!** Wear old clothing and make sure to protect your work area with newspaper, a drop cloth, or a tarp. Better yet, go outside!

- **Ask an adult** to help when using hot or sharp tools.

SCIENCE TERMS TO KNOW

CHEMISTRY (KEH-mis-tree): the study of matter

DENSITY (DEN-si-tee): the measure of a substance's volume compared to its mass

MEMBRANE (MEHM-brayn): a soft, thin layer of matter

MOLECULE (MOL-uh-kyool): two or more atoms bonded together

FOAMING SWAMP MONSTER

When molecules break up, things can get messy! Use chemistry to make a monster **spew slime and froth foam.**

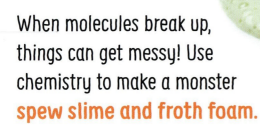

WHAT YOU NEED

- clean, empty can
- art supplies, such as felt, googly eyes & glue
- ½ cup (118 milliliters) hydrogen peroxide
- ¼ cup (59 mL) dish soap
- food coloring
- paper cup or other container for mixing
- mixing spoon
- active yeast
- ½ cup (118 mL) warm water
- measuring cups & spoons

6

WHAT YOU DO

STEP 1
Decorate a clean, empty can to look like a monster.

STEP 2
In the can, mix together the hydrogen peroxide, dish soap, and a few drops of food coloring.

STEP 3
In a separate container, mix together one packet of active yeast and the warm water. Let the mixture sit for at least five minutes.

STEP 4
Pour the yeast mixture into the can, and watch your monster foam!

WHAT YOU GET

A chemical reaction! Hydrogen peroxide is unstable. It wants to break into two parts, water and oxygen. This reaction normally takes time. But yeast causes the reaction to happen quickly. Dish soap captures the oxygen as it breaks from the hydrogen peroxide. This creates foam. **That's science!**

SLIME BUBBLES

This crystal-clear slime is just the beginning. What happens when you let your slime sit for a few days? Wait and see!

WHAT YOU NEED

- ½ cup (118 mL) clear school glue
- ¼ teaspoon (1.2 mL) baking soda
- saline contact solution containing boric acid
- mixing bowl & spoon
- measuring cups & spoons

WHAT YOU DO

STEP 1
Mix the clear school glue with the baking soda. Stir well.

STEP 2
Stir in the saline solution a few drops at a time until a ball forms. Coat your hands in saline solution and knead the ball until it becomes a smooth, nonsticky slime.

STEP 3

Set the slime aside. Let it sit covered for five to seven days.

WHAT YOU GET

Bubbles, baby! As the slime sits, air bubbles rise to the top. The slime is too thick for the air bubbles to escape right away. So, they form a layer on top. **That's science!**

HOT & COLD WATER STACK

Can you stack water without it mixing? Try to stay dry as you perfect this **topsy-turvy experiment!**

WHAT YOU NEED

- plastic container, such as a milk jug or soda bottle
- scissors or craft knife
- 2 glasses of the same size
- food coloring (2 colors)
- water
- mixing spoon

EXPERIMENT! TRY STACKING COLD WATER ON TOP OF HOT WATER. WHAT HAPPENS?

10

WHAT YOU DO

STEP 1
Cut a circle out of the plastic container. The circle should be big enough to completely cover the top of the glass.

STEP 2
Fill one glass with hot water. Stir in food coloring. Fill the other glass with cold water. Stir in a different color of food coloring.

STEP 3
Place the plastic circle on top of the hot-water glass. Carefully turn the glass over while holding the plastic firmly. Set the glass on top of the cold-water glass.

STEP 4
Carefully slide the plastic circle out from between the two glasses. Make sure to hold the top glass in place!

WHAT YOU GET

Density at work! Hot water is less dense than cold water. This allows the hot water to sit on top of the cold water without mixing in. **That's science!**

11

OOEY GOOEY ROCKS

Gather your glue and make some rock-filled slime that's ready to **roll onto the construction site.**

WHAT YOU NEED

- ⅔ cup (158 mL) clear school glue
- ½ cup (118 mL) liquid starch, plus extra
- pebbles
- mixing bowl & spoon
- measuring cups & spoons

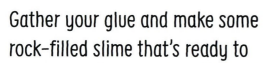

12

WHAT YOU DO

STEP 1
Stir together the clear school glue and liquid starch.

STEP 2
Add more liquid starch 1 tablespoon (15 mL) at a time until a ball forms. Knead the ball, adding starch as necessary until you have made a smooth, nonsticky slime.

STEP 3
Mix several dozen pebbles into the slime until the mixture can stand on its own.

WHAT YOU GET

Heavy-duty slime! The pebbles add mass to the slime, making it heavier. Heavier objects are pulled more strongly by gravity. So, the heavy slime moves in different ways than a lighter slime would. **That's science!**

GLITTER BOUNCY BALLS

Polymers are long chains of molecules. Rubber, plastic, and nylon are all polymers you probably use every day! Use polymers to make your own **sparkly bouncy balls!**

WHAT YOU NEED

- ¼ cup (59 mL) warm water
- 2 teaspoons (10 mL) borax
- paper cup
- ¼ cup (59 mL) school glue
- 4 teaspoons (20 mL) cornstarch
- food coloring
- glitter
- plate
- mixing bowl & spoon
- measuring cups & spoons

EXPERIMENT! TRY ADDING MORE OR LESS OF THE BORAX SOLUTION. WHAT HAPPENS?

WHAT YOU DO

STEP 1
Mix together the warm water and borax in a paper cup.

STEP 2
Mix together the school glue and cornstarch in a small bowl. Add food coloring and glitter to the mixture.

STEP 3
Add 2 teaspoons (10 mL) of the borax mixture to the glue mixture. Stir until it begins to solidify. Then, knead the mixture with your hands until a stiff dough forms.

STEP 4
Break off small chunks of dough and roll them into balls. The more you handle the dough, the stiffer it will get. Roll each ball in glitter. Then, give the balls a bounce! Store the balls in an airtight container when done using.

WHAT YOU GET

The power of polymers! The polymers in glue normally slide past each other. But the borax mixture makes the glue's polymers stick together. This causes the glue to become more solid and elastic. Cornstarch thickens the glue and helps the bouncy balls hold their shape. **That's science!**

CHALK BOMB

Harness the power of chemistry to make a colorful explosion. (This one is extra messy, so you may want to take it outside!)

MESS-O-METER: 6

WHAT YOU NEED

- colored sidewalk chalk
- plastic zipper-close bags
- hammer
- 1 tablespoon (15 mL) baking soda
- ¼ cup (59 mL) vinegar
- measuring cups & spoons

WHAT YOU DO

STEP 1
Place several pieces of chalk in a plastic bag. You can use just one color or combine colors!

STEP 2
Place the chalk bag on a hard surface, such as pavement. Use a hammer to smash the chalk into a fine powder.

STEP 3
If the bag is damaged from hammering, transfer the powder to a new bag. Add the baking soda to the bag.

STEP 4
Pour the vinegar into the bag and seal it tightly. Then, stand back and wait!

WHAT YOU GET

Kaboom! Sidewalk chalk and baking soda are bases. Vinegar is an acid. When the three substances mix, the acid causes the bases to release carbon dioxide. This gas expands until the bag explodes. **That's science!**

FIERCE FOUNTAIN

With just a balloon, a bottle, and a drinking straw, you can fashion a fierce fountain that spews colorful liquid. **Prepare to get wet!**

WHAT YOU NEED

- pushpin
- clear plastic water or soda bottle
- ballpoint pen
- drinking straw
- mounting putty
- water
- blue food coloring
- art supplies, such as a paper cup, duct tape, craft foam & more
- balloon

EXPERIMENT!
WHAT HAPPENS IF YOU MAKE THE WATER LEVEL HIGHER THAN THE STRAW?

18

WHAT YOU DO

STEP 1
Use a pushpin to poke a hole near the middle of a plastic water or soda bottle. Use a ballpoint pen to make the hole large enough for a drinking straw to fit through.

STEP 2
Insert the straw into the hole. Seal the seam between the bottle and straw with mounting putty.

STEP 3
Pour water into the bottle until it is just below the outer end of the straw. Add blue food coloring to color the water. Use a paper cup to decorate the end of the straw to look like a dragon or another animal.

STEP 4
Blow up a balloon. Keeping the end pinched closed, wrap the balloon opening around the mouth of the bottle. Stand back!

WHAT YOU GET

Air pressure at work! As the balloon deflates, its air rushes into the bottle. The force of the air pushes down on the water and forces it up through the straw. **That's science!**

EXPLODING WATERMELON

Grab your goggles and get ready for some wet and wild watermelon fun. Don't forget to enjoy a bite of melon **after the explosion!**

WHAT YOU NEED

- drop cloth or tarp (optional)
- eye protection
- watermelon
- rubber bands (about 100)

WHAT YOU DO

STEP 1
Spread out a tarp or drop cloth, if using, and put on eye protection.

STEP 2
Stretch a rubber band around the center of the watermelon.

STEP 3
Keep adding rubber bands. Pay attention as the watermelon changes shape and starts to bulge. Be patient! This may take time.

STEP 4
When you see the first large crack start to form in the melon, stand back. Your melon is about to blow!

WHAT YOU GET

Fruit under pressure! Each rubber band exerts a small amount of force on the melon. As you add more rubber bands, the force becomes greater. Eventually, it becomes so great that the melon explodes. **That's science!**

PAINT SPLATTER ART

You may want to dig out some old clothes for this art project. When paint and potential energy meet, **things will get messy!**

WHAT YOU NEED

- pushpins
- white tagboard
- tarp or drop cloth (optional)
- balloons
- funnel
- ¼ cup (59 mL) washable, nontoxic paint
- measuring cups & spoons

EXPERIMENT! TRY DROPPING THE BALLOON FROM DIFFERENT HEIGHTS. DOES IT CHANGE YOUR SPLATTER ART?

22

WHAT YOU DO

STEP 1
Insert pushpins through a white sheet of tagboard. Turn the tagboard over and place it pointy side up on a tarp, drop cloth, or grassy area that can get messy.

STEP 2
Stretch a balloon by inflating it and letting the air out. Insert a funnel into the end of the balloon. Pour the paint through the funnel and into the balloon.

STEP 3
Inflate the paint-filled balloon and tie the end.

Repeat **steps 2 and 3** to fill additional balloons.

STEP 4
Drop the balloons onto the pins and watch the paint splatter!

WHAT YOU GET

Energy in action! An inflated balloon stores potential energy. When the balloon pops, the potential energy converts into motion, sending the paint inside the balloon flying. **That's science!**

23

ICKY TAR PIT

Long ago, prehistoric animals became trapped in thick pools of tar. Create a special slime to mimic a dangerous tar pit!

WHAT YOU NEED

- 1 cup (0.24 liters) cornstarch
- ½ cup (118 mL) warm water
- black paint
- mixing bowl & spoon
- measuring cups & spoons
- plate
- plastic toys, sand & fake plants (optional)

EXPERIMENT! TRY ADDING MORE LIQUID OR LESS CORNSTARCH. WHAT HAPPENS?

24

WHAT YOU DO

STEP 1
Mix together the cornstarch and warm water.

STEP 2
Stir in a few tablespoons of black paint until the mixture is tar colored.

STEP 3
Continue stirring until the mixture thickens. Then, mix with your hands until you can squeeze the mixture into a ball.

STEP 4
Spread your "tar" out on a plate. If you like, add plastic toys, sand, and fake plants to your tar pit!

WHAT YOU GET

A non-Newtonian fluid! The substance you made isn't a liquid or a solid. When placed on top, toys sink as if into liquid. But if you poke or flick the substance, it feels solid. **That's science!**

COLOR-SHIFTING SLIME

Baby bottles, mood rings, and receipts all use thermochromic pigments to change color when exposed to heat. Mix up a batch of cool slime that gets even cooler **the warmer it gets.**

WHAT YOU NEED

- ¼ cup (59 mL) white school glue
- 1 tablespoon (15 mL) water
- food coloring (optional)
- 1 tablespoon (15 mL) thermochromic pigment
- ½ cup (118 mL) liquid starch
- mixing bowl & spoon
- measuring cups & spoons
- hot and cold items, such as a blow-dryer & ice pack

WHAT YOU DO

STEP 1
Stir together white school glue and water. Add food coloring if you'd like.

STEP 2
Add the thermochromic pigment to the mixture. Stir well.

STEP 3
Add ¼ cup (59 mL) of liquid starch. Stir to combine.

STEP 4
Add another ¼ cup (59 mL) of starch little by little. Knead the mixture until it is smooth, stretchy, and no longer sticks to your fingers.

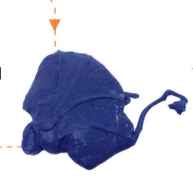

STEP 5
Change the temperature and color of your slime by using a blow-dryer, ice pack, and more!

WHAT YOU GET

Harnessed heat! Thermochromic pigment is made from special dyes or tiny crystals. When exposed to heat, the molecules in these substances change position. This causes the pigment to change color. **That's science!**

SCULPTABLE SAND

Mix up a batch of sand that you can mold, shape, and sculpt! What will you build?

WHAT YOU NEED

- ⅔ cup (158 mL) clear school glue
- ½ cup (118 mL) liquid starch, plus extra
- 1 cup (0.24 L) fine sand, plus extra
- mixing bowls & spoon
- measuring cups & spoons

28

WHAT YOU DO

STEP 1
Stir together the clear school glue and liquid starch.

STEP 2
Continue adding liquid starch 1 tablespoon (15 mL) at a time until a ball forms. Knead the ball, adding more starch as needed until it becomes a smooth and nonsticky slime.

STEP 3
In a separate bowl, use your hands to mix together the sand and half the slime. The mixture should be soft enough to mold but solid enough to hold a shape. Add more sand or slime until the mixture is the right consistency.

WHAT YOU GET

Flow like a liquid, squeeze like a solid! Mixing glue and starch makes a non-Newtonian slime. When the slime coats the sand, the sand acts like the slime. So, you can shape the sand into sculptures, blocks, and more. **That's science!**

SQUEEZE & SPLAT EGGS

With a little vinegar and a little time, you can turn a raw egg into a **smelly, bouncy, rubbery mess!**

WHAT YOU NEED

- clear plastic cups
- raw eggs
- vinegar
- food coloring
- white tagboard

EXPERIMENT!
LET YOUR EGGS SIT FOR DIFFERENT AMOUNTS OF TIME. HOW DOES THE EXPERIMENT CHANGE AS THE EGG SITS LONGER?

WHAT YOU DO

STEP 1

Place an egg into each cup. Add enough vinegar to each cup to cover the egg. Add a few drops of food coloring to the vinegar.

STEP 2
Let the eggs sit in the vinegar for three to seven days.

STEP 3
Remove the eggs from the cups. What do they feel like? Drop the eggs from different heights onto white tagboard. Do the eggs bounce or burst? What color are the yolks?

WHAT YOU GET

Colorful, rubbery eggs! Vinegar is acidic. It dissolves the hard part of the eggshell, leaving behind a soft, rubbery membrane. The colored vinegar flows through this membrane and colors the egg. But proteins in the egg yolk keep the yolk from absorbing any color. So, it stays yellow. **That's science!**

• • • • READ MORE • • • •

Leigh, Anna. *30-Minute Chemistry Projects*. Minneapolis: Lerner Publications, 2019.

Schuette, Sarah L. *10-Minute Science Projects*. North Mankato, MN: Capstone Press, 2020.

Weakland, Mark. *Kaboom!: Wile E. Coyote Experiments with Chemical Reactions.* North Mankato, MN: Capstone Press, 2017.

• • • • INTERNET SITES • • • •

Science Buddies—Chemistry Science Projects
sciencebuddies.org/science-fair-projects/project-ideas/chemistry

STEM Education Guide—Messy STEM Science Experiments for Kids
stemeducationguide.com/messy-stem-science-experiments-for-kids

Steve Spangler Science
stevespanglerscience.com